Why the Uni
Human Being Matters

The Doctrine of Body and Soul

Philip Miti
Doctoral Candidate at the
University of Heidelberg, Germany

GROVE BOOKS LIMITED
RIDLEY HALL RD CAMBRIDGE CB3 9HU

Contents

First Impression April 2025
ISSN 2633-8394
ISBN 978 1 78827 476 0

1 Introduction

Following the story of Joe, a black jazz musician who has a near-death experience, Pixar's 3D animated movie *Soul* mirrors back to us what our culture typically thinks about the nature of the body and its relationship with the soul. In the West, we tend to think of the body as a container or house. We imagine the soul as vapoury substance which lives inside the body without paying rent. In the film, Joe's soul leaves his body and eventually finds itself wandering among other souls. Many of these other souls either await insertion into earthly bodies or philosophize about the life they once had before being freed from their bodies. Although the film explores questions about life's meaning and purpose, it fails to give a full-blooded 3D (pun intended) account of Joe's own life which should include the earthly factors essential to his person.

We instinctively imagine soul and body in separation rather than unity

We instinctively imagine soul and body in separation rather than unity. On one side is a scientistic desire to reduce the whole world to atoms and material with little meaning or purpose beyond mechanisms and the movement of time. Here, the human is seen reductively and materialistically: it is a complex machine. The undeniable fact that we are conscious beings then, can only be seen as a problem, and a hard one at that. On the other side of the same coin, the human is a special being with a creative and powerful mind. Contemporary society seems increasingly comfortable with the idea of humans as 'spiritual' beings, as long as we remain vague about what spiritual means or which spirits influence us.

Furthermore, we have an ambivalent relation with our bodies today. It can be painful and/or popular to be dissatisfied with our bodies, particularly in an age in which we have turned ourselves into customers of our own body image and capabilities. Nevertheless, some bodies are not so easily commodifiable, such as disabled bodies. However, rather than energizing us towards proximity and mutual flourishing, people with disabilities become those from whom we hide our faces. This exposes our personal, ecclesial and societal values and confronts us with our limits. It also exposes who we think Jesus is and the value of his humanity. Whatever the case, it seems that we moderns are as uncomfortable with our limits as with our bodies and we project our hopes to overcome these limits on an idea of the soul. Whether through technologies, spiritual practices or scientific progress we seem committed to escaping our bodies, their natural pattern and givenness.

Most authoritative figures in the Christian tradition have approached the topic by prayerfully opening the Scriptures, listening to the wisdom of earlier Spirit-filled Christians as they read the Scriptures and remaining informed about the knowledge of their time. This certainly characterizes the approach of many of the figures mentioned in this book even if they do this in different ways. This book similarly starts by reflecting on Scripture with the help of ancient and contemporary Christians. However, the following chapters do not factor in enough voices such as your own to such a crucial conversation. Therefore, the questions which follow are meant both as an aid to those conversations which you may already be having and as a prompt for you own reflection.

Questions for Discussion

- Do you tend to order your words in this way, 'soul and body' or rather, 'body and soul'? Which way round feels more natural to you and why?
- When you pray, do you refer to your soul at all, like the Psalmist in Psalm 103, or perhaps, if you have ever sung Matt Redman's *10,000 Reasons*, what do you imagine visually?
- In what ways do you think modern Western societies and technologies have estranged us from our own (and each other's) bodies?
- What do you think the relationship might be between prayer, mindfulness and good mental health?

2

'Soul' in the Hebrew Bible

As modern people we might find it easy to imagine the soul resting in the body like air in an inflatable dust bag but the Hebrew Bible approaches the relationship between body and soul otherwise.

The Hebrew Bible starts its reflection about what humans are neither with an idea of what the body is like, nor the soul. It does not even start by asking what the human is. Rather it begins with the movement of the Spirit of God, the breath (*ruach*) of the living God. At the creation of humanity in Gen 2.7, God took dust and breathed into its nostrils and the human (*ha'adam*) became a living *soul* or living *creature* (*nephesh hayyah*).[1] We can thus note first off, that the Hebrew word for soul (*nephesh*) carries some physical connotations.

In the harshness of an arid desert climate where water is scarce, living things begin to wither. A merciless sun would shorten our breath and vitality, and our throats would dry up. This image introduces a second layer to the meaning of the Hebrew word for soul. Like a breathless deer who pants for water, reflects Psalm 42, so 'my *nephesh* (soul/throat) thirsts for you.' So we can note: on a practical level, *nephesh* can literally mean throat while figuratively meaning soul (Isa 58.11, Ps 23.3, Ps 42.1–2). This might seem unimportant at first until we think through what might be implied about its meaning.

- The throat (soul) is the physical connection between the head, heart and the whole body.
- Living existence depends upon the movement of breath (*ruach*-spirit) in, through and around the throat.
- Wind (*ruach*) animates the throat (larynx) to produce each unique voice.

Where *nephesh* does not mean throat in a literal way, it simply refers to the creature. However, taken alone, there is still something missing.

Turning to Song of Songs, thirdly, will help us to gather yet another important sense of the meaning of soul, *nephesh*. When the bride and groom in Song of Songs express their longing for one another, 'I have found the one whom my *nephesh* loves,' the point is that their love (beyond mere words) for one another moves each of them to give their *whole being* to the other (Song 3.4). Typically, the way English-speakers normally say soul refers to something inner and non-physical. But here, the bride and her groom desire to give one another their whole being (intimate connotations included!). They desire to become *one* just as their song is *one.*

The largely forgotten Old Testament scholar Aubrey R Johnson from Wales, described the human as a 'psychical whole' or a 'psycho-physical organism.'[2] In normal speak, he is saying that you do not *have* a soul; you *are* a soul. Because of their inextricable unity, to say 'soul' is already to imply body. Likewise, saying 'body' already implies soul. In much of the Hebrew Bible, soul implies one's whole creaturely existence.

Reflection

The singing voice does not only require the vocal chords; it is an act of the whole body, in which one's whole self is poured out in co-ordinated animated breathing. The lovers in Song of Songs pour themselves out in song implying that their whole bodies are involved in their passionate commitment to each other. Church liturgies generally aim at showing us that our bodies are an integral part of the song we sacrificially pour out to God together in union with him.

Activity

Try to notice your body, your position and your movements next time you are in church. Why do you kneel when you kneel? Is there space to kneel? Is there space for a wheelchair to move freely? What is the architecture trying to teach you about the relationship between your gaze and the cross of Christ? Who is afforded the most mobility in your church? What spiritual insights might be available to people with chronic pain for example, who are aware of their bodiliness in a way many of us disregard?

Song Suggestion

In cathedrals, John Lucas revitalizes the sense of awe that accompanies our bodily participation in the spaces which are dedicated to God whether that is a cathedral, home, the earth or green pastures. If you have access to the internet, feel free to give it a listen.

Bodily Limits and the New Testament

3

The Hebrew Bible presents a holistic portrait of the human being. Sure, but does it persist through the New Testament? In the late 1940s, New Testament scholar W D Davies argued that when Paul used the Greek word for soul, '*psychē*,' he had neither abandoned his Rabbinic Judaism nor the Hebrew Bible's holistic conception of soul in favour of Plato, Aristotle and the Greek Stoics.[3] He taught as a rabbi and his mind was immersed in the Hebrew Scriptures even though he was familiar with the Greek thinking of his context.

Paul was *not* a Greek dualist! This means that soul and body are not opposites or antagonists, but they echo each other as the self-same 'living creature' (Gen 2.7). When Paul used the word *psychē*—often translated *soul*—he was typically thinking about a whole concrete life which cannot abstracted from the body.

In her book *Body*, New Testament scholar Paula Gooder highlights biblical passages where bodily limits are portrayed as burdensome in Paul's Letter to the Romans. However, as she closely examines Paul's use of the language of flesh and body in Rom 7.24 and chapter 8 she unpacks how 'it is not the body that is the problem but the body laden with sin and death.'[4] The bounds imposed by sin and the power of death can be grievous because our bodies and souls were not made for sin. Rather, the body is meant 'for the Lord and the Lord for the body' (1 Cor 6.13).

Hence, it is the clear teaching of Scripture that our bodies are good, and that the body is a gift. This is why when Paul contrasts life 'according to the flesh' with life 'according to the Spirit,' the term *flesh* (*sarx*) in these instances does not refer to our bodiliness but our corruptibility and rebellion (Rom 8.1–4). Paul's use of the word flesh here (*sarx*) is not synonymous with the body (*sōma*). Life according to the Spirit is bodily-life lived unto God which is opposed to gratifying the sinful nature (Gal 5.16–17).

So What Does the New Testament Tell Us about the Relationship between Body and Soul?

Paula Gooder notes that in the New Testament, 'There is nowhere that Paul contrasts the word "soul" with the word "body."' The two are not enemies, they are one. The Greek philosopher Plato, on the contrary, saw the body as a coffin for the soul; a problem and limit without which we otherwise would be free. Plato believed that souls are good, but bodies are not great. This is not the teaching of the Bible, but popular and casual forms of this same dualism still haunt our culture today, affecting Christians as much as anyone else. This kind of dualism is certainly not a Christian mindset and it jeopardizes the gospel because it spurns the goodness of the incarnation!

God the Son came enfleshed, lived bodily among and in us, he touched and healed bodies, redeems bodies and he lives and reigns bodily even now! The New Testament reminds us that body and soul are good, that they matter and that they are somehow one.

> We are body and soul; created by the Lord and for the Lord.

Afterlife

A concise theology of 'afterlife' is of course impossible in a few sentences. It is striking that conceptions of the afterlife thrived in ancient Egypt and seem, on the contrary, foreign to the Hebrew Bible where the afterlife does not appear (at least not as we tend to mean it). For this reason, it is worth being cautious around this language. Thus, while Scripture more frequently speaks of the grave (Sheol), some Christians begin and ground their doctrine of the human being on the notion of an immortal soul. This is fraught with problems. The Scriptures are overwhelmingly clear that God is eternal, 'who alone is immortal and who lives in unapproachable light' (1 Tim 6.16). The human soul is not eternal in and of itself. Thus, even the exegetical arguments made from the New Testament for the notion of eternal punishment still must underline that the human is not immortal by nature (Matt 25.46). Those Christians who stress human mortality are right not to place their hope in the duality of human nature. As the Nicene Creed puts it, 'We (expect/look towards) the resurrection of the dead.'

The Human Spirit in Christian Tradition

4

The Human Spirit

But are we not forgetting spirit? In many modern British universities, between 1600 and 1800, the idea of the human spirit was sometimes confused with divine spirit. Generalized concepts of spirit were put to use, bridging the gap between divine and human. Often, the human body was seen as the place where they mix or meet. The main issue here concerns keeping these two distinct. Anglican theologian Ephraim Radner helps to sort through this confusion by pointing out how modern Christian reflection on the Spirit (pneumatology) wrongly became a subset of thinking about man (anthropology) or (in)visible things (creation). Accepting our human limits and frailties as a gift is as difficult today as it was conceptually then. Pneumatology as a university discipline became 'a modern invention' used as a way of escaping the frailty, violence and suffering of modern bodies.[5] Irish Anglican, bishop Robert Clayton's *Essay on Spirit* offers an example of the theology of the Spirit morphed into 'human projections or abstractions.'[6]

This was and is still a big mistake. It shrinks God by imagining him to be one of his own creatures. Put simply, the Holy Spirit is not the same as the human spirit.

The Human in Three Parts? On the Human Spirit

Early in the history of Christianity it was discussed whether there is a third part of the human alongside body and soul: the human spirit. Biblical passages such as 1 Thess 5.23 seem to suggest three parts. Nevertheless, we must always remember that body, soul and spirit are not like pieces of fabric which can be stitched or stuck together to make a human. A couple of important voices from the Christian tradition have wise advice for us:

- First, the North African bishop St Augustine (354–430) notes that it is best not to get distracted when one reads of the 'human spirit' in Scripture. This is because the words spirit and soul are often used interchangeably. 'Of these three, one is quite different, such that we can call them two.'[7] So the human *is* body and soul. The human is *nephesh*. But the human also *has* spirit. But what does it mean that we *have* spirit?

- Early African Father, Tertullian (155–220), who wrote the first full Christian treatise, *On the Soul*, helps us make sense of the sentence, 'humans have spirit.' Wisely, his thought process begins not with humans but with the living God. This is a good habit for theological thinking because if God himself is the living one, we are reminded that we depend entirely on him for every breath and every word about him. Theologian Katherine Sonderegger examples this, always returning to how Scripture reveals the holy and fiery livingness of God. Quite like Tertullian, she grasps that God is Spirit (John 4.24) and that God is sheer life (Exod 3.14, John 11.25).[8] We are not. We humans on the other hand are *made* to be alive. To say that we *have* spirit is to reflect on the way that we receive the gift of living by the Spirit who *is* life. The Spirit should not be seen as a piece of human nature or an ability. Similarly, we do normally talk of life as if it is one of our organs or a mere ability. Rather, 'in him we live and move and have our being' (Acts 17.28). Tertullian emphasized the unity of body and soul concluding that, 'for [the human] to live is to breathe and to breathe is to live.'[9]
- God is life! What lies otherwise void and dead in dust is made alive by God through the living word in the power of the Spirit. Every *nephesh* depends completely on God for life. In the words of theologian David Kelsey, we are 'living on borrowed breath.'[10] This is a message of hope, because it means that 'man lives and dies in the livingness of God.' Talk of body and soul is therefore non-reductive. Even in death, the creature is a living witness to the God who is life itself!

Furthermore, the Hebrew Bible presents humans as complex beings and offers a rather sophisticated psychology. Its basic message: we are *whole* beings and we are only whole in and through the God who gives us life. He is merciful to preserve life, he is just in taking it back from us and he is the redeemer of life.

A Much Too Brief Reformation Theology of the (Ensouled) Body

5

John Calvin on the Heart

The French theologian and reformer John Calvin (1509–1564), sealed his written letters with a motto: '*cor meum tibi offero domine prompte et sincere* (my heart I offer to you Lord, promptly and sincerely).'[11]

Contrary to (some) unfortunate popular prejudices, the tone of Calvin's theology is rather gentle and comforting. Applying the gospel like a salve upon the tender soul, faithful readers will find in Calvin's writing a theology addressed to the restless heart. It preaches to the believer the consoling guarantee of adoption in Christ through the life-giving Spirit, all under the loving fatherly providence of God. The pessimism that many people discover in Calvin's caricature is really his refusal to entrust the human heart with the burden of redeeming itself from its own disorder. The basic message is that all of God's children can know all the benefits and comfort of Christ's redeeming work. However, this lies beyond our grasp and is not given to us on the basis of spiritual self-defibrillation. There is no way to reanimate a dead heart through human works; rather it is the power of the gospel to penetrate to 'the inmost affections of the heart, fix its seat in the soul and pervade the whole man' (III.6.4).

The Intellectual Soul as the Seat of the Image of God

Calvin's account is both beautiful and truthful. However, it leaves us in the dark as to the relation between heart, soul and body. Early in his work, Calvin prioritizes the soul, honouring it as the 'nobler part.' He believed that the soul is where the image of God sits. In *Institutes of the Christian Religion*, Calvin couples this positive view of the soul with its powers: 'The soul of man possesses reason, intellect, and will—qualities which are not annexed to the body.'[12] He suggested that what makes us human is the capacity (*facultas*) for reason, intellect and will but there is a problem here. Although this is not Calvin's main point about human purpose, it does suggest that mental faculties are implied in what it means to image God by reflecting God's own attributes. As one can imagine, this coupling of intellectual powers with the image of God is laden with problematic logical consequences challenged outright by the full and exemplary humanity of people with cognitive disabilities. Thus, here Calvin's logic deserves cautious attention.

Furthermore, when Calvin likened God's non-bodiliness with the human soul's non-physicality, he brought these similarities unhelpfully close together. He marvelled at our human soul's capacity for contemplation, memory and thought, describing these wonders of the soul as 'unfailing signs of divinity in man.'[13] In his recent work, the *Logic of the Body,* Matthew A Lapine helps us challenge Calvin on the importance of the body in humanness, 'Calvin does admit that the whole human being is body and soul but seems to imply that the body is of no concern in spiritual matters.'[14] Calvin regrettably neglected the body and focussed on the soul and its powers.

The Soul as the Nobler Part?

Neglect of the body feeds into Calvin's conception of the interrelation of soul and body. Following Aristotle, he understood the soul to be the dominant part, responsible for animating and governing the body. At points one can detect a deep antagonism in the relationship between body and soul as if the presence of these two distinct substances was always bound for friction. Nevertheless, though Calvin's nobler part (soul) chafes against the lesser part (body), the lack of theological attention given to the body in the *Institutes* by no means implies disdain for the body. On the contrary, Calvin holds the body's design in high esteem. It 'shows itself to be a composition so ingenious that its artificer is rightly judged a wonder-worker.'[15] Calvin marvels at the wonder of the human body. He is moved to awe and praise of the wondrous creator.

Here Calvin does much better than one of his followers, the (normally and otherwise) honey-mouthed preacher and Anglican theologian Richard Sibbes (1577–1635), who wrote, 'The best men's bodies in this world are vile.' That does not sound right, and it is not. The reader, quite desperate for Sibbes to better explain himself, waits in vain for him to self-correct. Instead, he strays deeper into the same error, writing that the human is, 'vile in regard of the matter whence they are taken, from the dust. The fairest body is but well coloured dust.'[16] Facepalm! Much of Sibbes' work is on the contrary wonderful and commendable, but his persistent denigration of the body in this particular treatise is simply contrary to Scripture and a poor example of the Reformed tradition's doctrine of humanity!

Immortality and the Heart

Calvin's tendency to elevate the soul over the body was likely motivated by his commitment to defending the soul's immortality. Whether this elevation is necessary is debatable and it may well reflect his own philosophical crutches particularly as he tries to articulate what the soul is. His most basic definition of the soul is:

> ...an 'incorporeal substance' which is non-spatial, immortal and 'housed in the body.'[17]

- The housing image is rather unfortunate not only because it is stolen from Plato—who used it even less than Calvin did—but because this image is alien to the Hebrew Bible. A significant amount of the theoretical heavy lifting in Calvin's commitment to the soul's immortality is done by Greek philosophers such as Cicero and Plato; not to mention how much he (and many protestant reformers) inherited Aristotle's philosophy of body-soul unity (hylomorphism). In fact, Calvin only really gets allergic to Aristotle where Aristotle himself implies that the soul is *not* immortal but bound to the body, a perfectly legitimate philosophical and theological position to hold.
- Despite his love for Scripture, Calvin's use of the Hebrew Bible on the soul in *Institutes* is limited to Eccl 12.7 and Job 4.19.[18] Calvin seems to let the proof texts and the philosophers interpret each other rather than contributing a fully fleshed-out biblical anthropology.

One can safely conclude that Calvin, in his early career, 'wanted to be biblical in his approach to psychology rather than philosophical.'[19] However, despite his dedication to reading the world through the spectacles of Scripture, Calvin's doctrine of body, soul and immortality were filtered heavily through Platonist/Aristotelean Greek philosophical lenses.

Wisdom from the Lutheran Approach

The German reformer, Martin Luther (1483–1546) was more reluctant to give the philosophers space on this matter. The Lutheran tradition, broadly speaking, has been stricter and more cautious about where and when philosophical reason can be used.[20] Where the use of reason stands over Scripture rather than kneeling before its claims the clear teaching of the gospel is jeopardized. Martin Luther believed that neither the soul's immortality nor the body's resurrection can be judged by human reason. Rather, the immortality of the soul is a confession. Its basis is confessional and not philosophical. Just as the resurrection of the body is an article of faith, so is the soul's immortality. We believe it only because God revealed these things to us in Scripture and we place hope regarding our continuation not on the basis of any philosophical impulse but simply because of God's promise. This view was echoed by many other Orthodox Lutherans such as Andreas Musculus (1514–1581) and Johann Gerhard (1582–1637).[21]

It must be said that Lutheran theologians were not (all) averse to borrowing philosophical language (including Luther), though it tended to be Aristotle's rather than Plato's. Luther's own protégé Philipp Melanchthon saw things differently to Luther and in his very Aristotelian work *On the Soul* tried to establish the soul's immortality. Accepting the diversity of approaches within orthodox Protestantism, we learn from the Lutheran tradition not to abstract the doctrine of body and soul from the living hope which neither perishes nor fades but is its anchor (1 Pet 1.3–4). In other words, there might be purchase in talking philosophically about body and soul, but it likely also simultaneously discloses and conceals some other alien hopes native to that particular philosophy.

It falls to us to amend Calvin's thought with some of his own better biblical instincts. Calvin's influential theological psychology of the heart and its relation to the unity of body and soul has been very influential but it is not entirely consistent. Scripture uses the word heart in so many different ways that Calvin's inconsistent use of the word heart is actually quite biblical, lacking perhaps only confidence. In Scripture, the heart often refers to what we now call mind, but it also sometimes means the will (which is one of the soul's faculties) and occasionally heart refers to the soul itself. The heart both keeps us living while being the organ of thinking and discernment (Ps 14.1). Thoughts are registered and emotions reside in the heart. The heart is the centre of cognition and as such it has intentions (Heb 4.12) the mouth speaks out of it (Luke 6.45), it desires (2 Sam 7.3; Ps 37.4) can be deceitful (Jer 17.9), joyful (Judg 16.25; Ps 104.15; Prov 17.22), it can be broken and can be a store of evil (Luke 6.45). The heart can be transformed (Ezek 36.26).

Scripture uses each organ to present a holistic portrait of the human being

Scripture is doing something more sophisticated than a basic human anatomy or systematic theory. It uses each organ to present a coherent holistic portrait of the human being. Thus, to love our Lord with soul, might, strength and mind reflects not division in the human constitution but rather unity before God in true worship (Mark 12.33). The Scriptures utilize these distinctions to emphasize unity not separation.

Worship concretizes our life before God as one whole life, body and soul, one sacrifice of praise. It is the lifting up and transformation of our hearts in worship that typifies the 'whole life or *nephesh*' which rises as an offering to God, materially transformed through the fire of God's glory (Leviticus 9; Matt 26.6–13).[22] This illuminates the wisdom of Calvin's motto, 'My heart I offer to you Lord sacrificially, promptly and sincerely' (Rom 12.1–2).

Karl Barth and Dietrich Bonhoeffer on Body and Soul 6

'You don't have a soul. You are a soul. You have a body.'[23]
George Macdonald (falsely attributed to C S Lewis)

Greek body-soul dualisms helped many pre-and-post-Reformation Christians justify the immortality of the soul. This arguably helped to solve some theological problems, while creating new ones. Where the Christian hope is at stake, one must tread cautiously if one wishes to resource Western philosophies. Granted, we must always discern where philosophy's sharp incisiveness is but a blunt theological hammering, but it would be unwise to write off the use of philosophy entirely. In fact, the Christian tradition's body-soul doctrine has been expressed with and through the languages and philosophies available to it throughout the ages.

With more space, this booklet would have considered the fruitful ways philosophy has been commandeered and put to theological work. The heavenly teacher Thomas Aquinas (1225–1274), for example, defends the idea of the 'living soul' using Aristotle's writings. The *soul* gives life and order to the *matter* of the body. The soul is not a mere part of the body like an organ, but neither does it float above the body separate from it. This rational soul needs the body and cannot think without bodily organs like the brain and gut. Aquinas offered a theory of human thinking which treats the body as an integrated whole, not just a disembodied mind, an insight which today's psychologists are rediscovering right now! Gregory of Nyssa (335–c 384) bends Greek philosophical terms, ideas and even Plato's whole work *Timaeus* to the service of a theology of human being. Envisioning how death has become subservient to life in the believer, he reflects on 1 Cor 15.31 and what it means to die daily.[24]

Humankind is Materially Constituted

While he was still young, theologian Willie James Jennings's mother would wrap her son's little hands within her own and submerge them deep into the soil in their garden. Under the gaze of motherly affection Willie's hands were among the earliest sites of his theological education.[25] Between his fingers he felt Scripture's teaching about the fashioning of all fleshly creatures and *the earth* (*ha'adamah*) from which *the humanity (ha'adam)* was taken and formed in Genesis. Meditating on the nothingness of human existence apart from the creating word of God and the soil from which we came, the German theologian Dietrich Bonhoeffer (1906–1945) composed an attentive theological exposition of Chapters 1—4 of Genesis.[26] His figural exegesis of Eph 5.14 offers a window into his reading of Gen 2.7: 'the word of God the almighty once summoned humankind out of the earth in which it was sleeping, in which it was dead and indeed a mere piece of earth, but a piece of earth called by God to have human existence.'[27] Bonhoeffer also reminds us that it is God's blessed ground out which our bodies come, not cursed ground. He continues in a way which corrects George MacDonald's quotation considerably, 'A human being does not "have" a body or "have" a soul; instead, a human being "is" body and soul,' in its unity and integrity.[28]

To separate body and soul, to set one over the other or to undermine their togetherness is a way of dehumanizing people in Bonhoeffer's view. He was also nervous about people's obsession with *ideas* about humanness. Mere ideas of human identity cannot replace encounter with real humans. Bonhoeffer's thought helps divert undue attention from our ideas of what human means as if mere ideas could draw us nearer to humanity than other humans could. Trying to cram real concrete humanity into ideas is a kind of spiritual violence. On the contrary, we can only start with and accept the concreteness and givenness of bodies (ours and others). This honours our neighbour, and it honours God: 'People who reject their bodies reject their existence before God the creator.'[29]

The Spirit is the Basis of Body and Soul

For many modern people it is counterintuitive to imagine that the Holy Spirit who is *immaterial* could be the constitutive basis for *material things* such as our physical bodies. Yet the directionality of Bonhoeffer's thought *from* God the Spirit *towards* creation is wise. It stresses that the human 'really does live only by God's spirit; that is what constitutes its essential being.'[30] His Swiss friend Karl Barth would speak in similar terms, asserting that the Spirit is the basis of soul and body. Only in this way can one say, 'the human has Spirit' and only because of this can one say, 'the human exists.' Note that Barth does not ground the notion of existence in terms of Greek philosophy. Rather, whatever existence is, it is the work of God the Spirit through the word of the Father Almighty: 'When we say "human" or "soul and body" then unwittingly we have first said "God"' because God is holy and eternally the *living* one.[31] With Gen 1.2 and 3.19 in mind, Barth summarizes that God does not need humans to be God. We are utterly dependent upon him for life, existence and sustenance. That the Spirit is given at all is permission to live, and the lack of the spirit is death:[32] One can reiterate with chapter three, thus, that the Spirit is not a third thing alongside body and soul any more than *life* is one of our organs.

Barth wrote that as the basis of soul and body, the living Spirit grounds, maintains and constitutes the human soul and body. He then refers to the human as soul-of-their-body.[33] For Barth there is no way to talk about the human as soul-of-their-body by first dividing them on the basis of a philosophical principle such as indivisibility (Descartes) or even immortality (Plato). In other words, trying to grasp hold of humanness through dead abstract ideas about body and soul reflects a misplaced hope. It attempts to cut past the work of the living Spirit, the one who grounds, maintains and constitutes us. Truly death itself is more concrete than these abstract categories. Yet death itself is but an 'impressive reminder that even as a body, the human does not belong to herself. Even as bodily, life is a matter which does not rest in our hands, but in the hands of God.'[34] As far as Barth was concerned, Descartes' dualism draws an abstract cut-out cartoon of the human on philosophical paper. Then using the concept of *di-visibility* as philosophical scissors, it proceeds to cut the human out so that it is both divisible (body) and indivisible (soul). But in the end, the nature of both substances is determined by the snipping of the scissors, 'two parts inadequately glued together.'[35] This also leaves us unsure as to how truthful that cut-out really was in the first place.

Phew! That was a bit of a mental gymnastics, but it prepares us well to explore briefly what Barth makes of the interconnexion of body and soul. We have already learnt that Barth considers the humans to be a whole. He is not interested in abstract dualisms but rather the concreteness of human life grounded, maintained and constituted by the Spirit. This is why Barth's nervousness about abstraction went as far as language. Many theologians are happy to refer to body and soul as substances. Barth was not one of them. Rather, picking up on the language of the overlooked Reformed systematic theologian, Eduard Böhl (1836–1903), body and soul are to be considered *moments*.[36] They are 'two moments of an indivisibly one human nature.'[37] Hence, we cannot be talking about body unless we already imply that it is the body of the soul. You are the embodied soul of your ensouled body. In the totality of these two moments, we live, move and have being. Let us conclude with a couple of considerations.

A Holistic Psychology

- For Barth, whatever subjectivity is it must be thought through theologically. Subjectivity does not arise out of an instance of autonomous mental action or out of the complexity of the human brain. If this would define and determine what it means to be a subject, human subjectivity would be closed-off, unperceptive and certainly not free—not to mention the impact of sin upon human nature! It is God's relation to the human through the Spirit that makes it a subject. Being bound to God and to our neighbour is precisely what *increases* freedom and subjectivity, odd as that may sound. To be more tightly bound to God and his ways is to live ever more deeply in communion and fellowship and therefore freedom.

- This is first because God is free, and his freedom does not compete with human freedoms. Secondly, because we do not exist for ourselves: we are not made to be self-centred; in fact this is a result of the sinfulness of fallen human nature. St Augustine and Martin Luther describe our tragic egocentric condition as the heart curved-in-on-itself. Autonomous life is self-determined (self-entrapped) life, just like the humans who took and ate from the tree of the knowledge of good and evil for themselves. However, 'in(ter)dependent life is not for itself.'[38] We are literally made to be outward facing or 'ex-centric' towards God, each other and the world.

Before we can speak in psychological or philosophical terms about subjectivity, we stand before God and in relation to him. Only then can we begin to speak about subjectivity because God personally created us body and soul. Not as soul or body but 'in the unity and totality of the two' are our lives entrusted and accorded to us to meet God and stand before him.[39]

Conclusion

There is a shift in contemporary cognitive psychology and psychotherapy towards more holistic models of human mental life. Disenchanted with more abstract dualist or representational models of human cognition, the *embodied cognition* paradigm in psychology takes whole body into account as it informs all levels of cognition. Tobias Tanton's *Corporeal Theology* is among the first theological books to engage with embodied cognition with serious depth, tackling its implications for how God speaks to us, church life and liturgical practice.[40] This arrives at a time where theology is also learning to pay attention to how trauma is not simply the abstract mental recollection of horrifying memories but repeats itself in bodily relived experience. Furthermore, among the many things the sacraments of baptism and eucharist teach us, we learn: (1) that it is through the body that we come to know and participate in sin and its effects. However, we also learn (2) that the body is the site of revelation. If God's posture toward us is the basis for our subjectivity, revelation can never simply be conceived of as a transfer of information or simply stored knowledge *about* God as if we were walking USB sticks. We *matter* to God because the act of creation is a *personal* matter. Bodies matter to God. Indeed, he makes himself known to our bodies through the body of Jesus Christ.

7 The Resurrection of Machines? Rowan Williams and Athenagoras

In his treatise *On the Resurrection* (*De Resurrectione*) Athenagoras of Athens (~133–90 CE), one of the earliest Church Fathers, asked an unusual question about how the soul keeps its immortality: 'If a human being consumes an animal that itself had consumed a human being, how will God keep the parts straight at the resurrection (Res 4)?' Will God sort out which cells and parts belong to each body like M&Ms or a jigsaw puzzle? And how will the souls remain immortal? We can complicate this situation further with the well-known fact that only 43% of the cells in your body are even human cells in the first place; the rest of our cells are bacterial.[41] Is a human soul, only the soul of the 43%? How will my identity survive death into the resurrection? What will brain function be like in the resurrection? In chapter four we explored the implications of being *one whole* organism, as body and soul. There is tighter unity between the eye and thought, diet and mental health, mind and the brain etc, than we typically assume.

Neuroscientists and psychologists have got us all talking about the wonders of the brain, its incredible design and organization and how this organ is crucial to who we are. However, since the 1970s we keep talking about our brains, minds and even the unconscious with the same concepts we use for computers and robots. We talk of emotional processing, problem-solving,' our memories are encoded, stored or sometimes saved in our brains which collect information/data and we are hard-wired to think and behave in certain ways etc. This makes up a lot of our everyday language about ourselves. The brain is conceived by many scientists as an organic machine, the result of a complex mechanical world process of evolution. The mind/consciousness (like software) emerges from the complexity of the machinery of the brain (hardware). We have made an industry out of the machine metaphor, and it makes intuitive sense to us. However, Rowan Williams points out rather sharply in his book, *Being Human*, that machines cannot make mistakes; they can only malfunction.[42] In order to recognize a mistake, the machine would need to have conscious viewpoint which is itself not already a product of the same mistake. Computers are intelligent only in the way they blindly do what they are told until there is a programming bug. On the other hand, the ability you and I have to be *truly* mistaken is the real sign of intelligence.

The brain is conceived by many scientists as an organic machine

There is a long-standing movement of psychologists who are dissatisfied with the machine-based language we use to refer to the living organisms we are. Furthermore, they think that a more embodied approach to human cognition might help us make sense of the brain as part of the body and mental life as something bodily rather than above or beyond the body. On the role of the body in knowing, Rowan Williams puts it thus, 'If the mind is emphatically something we learn about *as bodies*, the very notion of the body takes for granted something about the mind.'[43] Williams turns briefly to *Book VII* of *Confessions* in which St Augustine talks of his struggles to attain spiritual knowledge. His devotion to 'mental abstractions and inwardness' brought him to eternal truths yet failed miserably to change his habits.[44] Renouncing the search for abstract mystical help from up in an imagined sky, Augustine 'finally gave himself up to the Christian faith, throwing himself down, he says on the embodied divinity that was stretched out at his feet—the human narrative of Jesus Christ.'[45]

According to Augustine, the way 'to learn anything about the Spirit, the spiritual realm, let alone God, involves a way down. It involves a recognition of one's own mortality and physicality,' perhaps also one's limits and disability.[46] The Christian life reaps growth in the practical intelligence of listening attentively, discernment in self-examination, study and digestion of the Scriptures, being given to love and charity, lamenting boldly, fostering community, resisting temptation, imagining with discipline, being slow to speak, thinking scientifically, praying daily, practising dying, resting healthily and more. Few of these are solitary. All of these are bodily. If prayer is indeed 'the chief exercise of faith,' then this too is exercised in humility, from humus—the earth out of which hum-an is made.[47] The human indeed is an earth creature (chapter two); a plant if you will. This is what Willie Jenning's mother taught her son submerging his hands in their garden soil (see chapter four).

Humans are frequently referred to as trees/ fruiting plants in Scripture

Perhaps we have too quickly dismissed one of Scripture's most prominent ways to talk about human beings. Humans are frequently referred to as trees/fruiting plants in Scripture.[48] They are paralleled in ways which go beyond a mere descriptive simile or metaphor. In the creation narrative of Gen 2.3–31 God *planted* the Eden-garden. Humans and trees are placed there. The literary design pairs them symmetrically on day 3 and day 6. They both produce seed which lives beyond themselves, they both rise from the ground (day 3) and are both made to bear fruit (day 6). This theme is further developed in Isaiah 55 and reflected Ps 1.1–6 and Ps 92.12–61 where righteousness is the fruit of a flourishing tree (see also Ezek 17.5, 24; 1 Chron 16.33; Isa 44.3, 61.3, 65.22; Jer 17.7–8, 23.5; Prov

11.30). Furthermore, the coming messiah is foretold in Isaiah 11 as a shoot from whose roots a branch will bear fruit (Isa 11.1). In the New Testament: Jesus taught that he is the true vine in John 15, he cursed the fig tree for not producing fruit in Matthew 21.18f. There are countless biblical examples which demand fresh attention. Books such as Matthew Sleeth's *Reforesting Faith* offer a superb pastoral introduction.[49]

Scripture implores us to think of human beings and human vocation using trees and not just metaphorically. What if we trusted these more-than-metaphors when it came to questions about body and soul, resurrection, death and identity? Athenagoras' question about human fate did not come from an anxious place. This is because he does not start out by *first* thinking about the nature or the continuity of body and soul and *then only afterwards*, with fingers crossed, begin to think of the resurrection. His thinking goes in the other direction! 'If there is no resurrection, human nature is no longer genuinely human.'[50] For him, it is the resurrection that determines what it means to be human. *The end determines the beginning!* The meaning and nature of body and soul is already founded on the incarnate crucified Lord. If we want to understand what the human as body and soul *means*, we must start with this one who *is* the tree of life, who says 'Take, eat, this is my body.'

Jesus refers to himself as a plant, pointing directly to crucifixion

The New Testament encourages us to look for the risen messiah. In John 12.24, Jesus refers to himself as a plant, pointing directly to what his body was to achieve for us at his crucifixion. 'Very truly I tell you, unless a kernel of wheat falls to the ground and dies, it remains only a single seed. But if it dies, it produces many seeds (NIV).' Paul sounded very similar in response to the Corinthian crowd who questioned the nature of bodies in the resurrection in 1 Cor 15.35. 'But someone will ask, "How are the dead raised? With what kind of body do they come?" Fool! What you sow does not come to life unless it dies. And as for what you sow, you do not sow the body that is to be, but a bare seed, perhaps of wheat or of some other grain. But God gives it a body as he has chosen, and to each kind of seed its own body' (1 Cor 15.35–38; NRSV).

So, the resurrection bodies we await will be 'spiritual bodies' and therefore not physical right? No! Paula Gooder puts it well: 'We do not look forward to redemption *from* our bodies but to the redemption *of* our bodies.'[51]

It might be that in the new heavens and the new earth, our resurrection bodies will still consist of mostly (good?) bacteria. There are many Christians who would like to know if resurrection will change or remove their disabilities. For other Christians who live with disability, this is simply not a question. The fact that Jesus' resurrection body still bears the wounds of crucifixion leaves a lot of food for thought in the light of present suffering and all of us who struggle with our wounds or disabilities. All of these questions about what is continuous in the transformation of our bodies, and what is discontinuous, about the nature of body and soul are wasted on machinery imagery. These questions birth better questions when asked in the context of Scripture's narrative and imagery: We expect the seeds we bury in their earthy graves to transform physically. The growing tree looks nothing like the seed it came from; it lives fully in a way which the seed cannot. The seed is nevertheless beautiful, important and the material basis for the tree. Without the seed there could be no tree. Just wind. Similarly, our bodies, our lives must be transformed through death. We offer our bodies up to the Lord as a living sacrifice. Our lives are transformed through death even now, so that we live the resurrection life now in the Spirit.

In the light of the anxieties we have about our current bodies, the lies we have been told about our resurrection bodies and the hopes we have about the life to come it is the risen crucified body of the messiah upon whom our gaze must remain fixed. In a personal conversation with Brian Brock, Professor of Moral and Practical Theology at the University of Aberdeen, he once said (much more eloquently) to me, 'We can rest assured in the new heavens and the new earth, that there no more will be whatever hinders us now from the worship and presence of God.' I took it to apply also to what we often call disabilities now, which might before God be signs of his glory. Furthermore, I was challenged to reflect on the ways in which some of my own able-bodied capabilities, mental capacities, supposed freedoms and passions are the very hindrances which will be no longer in the new creation.

8

Conclusion

In chapter three, we briefly mentioned Song of Songs; the drama between a bride and her groom as they pine for union: '…when I found him whom my soul loves. I held him and would not let him go.' We have by now learnt to read 'my soul' in Hebrew, not cheaply as an immaterial thingamajig residing inside a shell called the body. Rather 'my soul (*nephesh*)' means 'my whole being (body and soul).' The implications are physical and bodily and more.

Early theologian Origen (185–253) was controversially accused of having a similar doctrine of body and soul to the Pixar film mentioned in the introduction. God supposedly injected pre-existent souls into fresh bodies and sent them as punishment to earth until their bodies died there and the souls went back to God. Close attention, however, reveals that Origen did not really hold this view. His notion of pre-existence or a pre-existent church rather was trying to communicate that the love of God for his people is so magnificent and immovable that you will never find the groom without his bride, nor Christ without his cross. In Christ, God and humanity are united!

What kind of love eagerly forgoes bodily presence?

Similarly, Athenagoras, in chapter six, reads our reality in light of the end; Adam in the light of Christ! Origen contemplated the eternal groom (Christ) united in steadfast love to his bride (church) in an unquenchable love, a love which is stronger than time, stronger than sin, stronger than death: but what kind of love can be fulfilled at a distance? And what kind of love eagerly forgoes bodily presence? Certainly not the love of God for us revealed at the cross of Jesus Christ! Song of Songs is no mere ancient Romeo and Juliet. It is about the love of God for his people. As far as Origen is concerned, one does not simply meander into Song of Songs! Envisioning Scripture as spiritual temple he saw the Song of Songs as the holy of holies, right at the centre.[52] We enter into the presence of God, through Christ to whom we are united. In him as an offering through death towards life the soul finds itself united most intimately with God as we at our final death with transformed body and soul rise like a song of all songs to him who has come down to us!

For a sweeping summary, the first two chapters highlight Scripture's vision of the unity of body and soul, highlighting some unfamiliar yet important images. For example, the notion that the human voice is one organic whole, no less physical than it is invisible. Likewise, the Hebrew word for soul also means *throat* and bears both physical and spiritual connotations. To lift one's voice to the heavens in a song of praise, wind (Spirit) must animate the vocal cords (physical matter), pouring through the throat to create a unique voice. Chapter four continues this tune, teasing out the implications of John Calvin's biblical theology of the heart. The chapter begins and ends with Calvin's (and our) song of ascent, 'My heart I offer to you Lord sacrificially, promptly and sincerely.' In chapter five, Bonhoeffer and Barth addressed the neglect of the doctrine in the twentieth century. Taking the focus off the capacities of the individual they emphasized the life of God from whom the human comes to be and live. Having addressed the *what* and the *who* of body and soul, chapters six and seven highlight the utter dependence of human life upon God. The *meaning* of body and soul only becomes apparent as we give ourselves up wholly to God (Matt 16.24–26). This is what is made clear in the Bible's tree imagery throughout Scripture. Seeds do not just morph into trees, they must first be buried in the grave of the earth becoming nothing…And God loves to create out of that which is nothing.

Bibliography

K Barth, *Church Dogmatics III/2* (G W Bromiley, T F Torrance (eds), (trans) G W Bromiley, H Knight, J K Reid and R H Fuller) (Edinburgh: T and T Clark, 1960, second edition).

'Be Not Entangled again in a Yoke of Bondage,' *The British Friend*, 1(1), 158 (July 1892).

J Behr, 'Nature Makes an Ascent from the Lower to the Higher: Gregory of Nyssa on Human Distinctiveness,' *Zygon*, 58(2), 2023, 539-553.

E Böhl, *Dogmatik* (T Schirrmacher (ed)) (Bonn: Reformatorischer Verlag, 2019).

D Bonhoeffer, *Creation and Fall* (Vol 3) (J De Gruchy (ed), and (trans) D S Bax) (Minneapolis, MN: United States of America: Fortress Press, 2004).

J Calvin, *Ioannis Calvini Opera quae supersunt omnia: Epistolicus Calvianus* (Vol IX) (trans G Baum) (Saxony: C A Schwetschke et filium, 1873).

J Calvin, *Institutes of the Christian Religion* (Vol 1) (J T McNeill (ed), and (trans) F Lewis Battles) (Louisville, KY: Westminster John Knox Press, 1960).

J Calvin, *Institutes of the Christian Religion* (Vol 2) (J T McNeill (ed), and (trans) F Lewis Battles) (Louisville, KY: Westminster John Knox Press, 1960).

W D Davies, *Paul and Rabbinic Judaism: Some Rabbinic Elements in Pauline Theology* (London: SPCK, 1979, third edition).

P Gooder, *Body: Biblical Spirituality for the Whole Person* (London: SPCK, 2016).

W J Jennings, *The Christian Imagination: Theology and The Origins of Race* (New Haven, CT: Yale University Press, 2010).

A R Johnson, *The Vitalilty of the Individual in the Thought of Ancient Israel* (Cardiff: University of Wales Press, 1964, second edition).

D Kelsey, *Eccentric Existence* (Vol 1) (Louisville, KY: Westminster John Knox Press, 2009).

M A Lapine, *The Logic of the Body: Retrieving Theological Psychology* (Bellingham, WA: Lexham Press, 2020).

R P Lawson, *Origen: The Song of Songs Commentary and Homilies* (Westminster, MD: Newman Press (1957).

E Radner, *A Profound Ignorance: Modern Pneumatology and its Anti-modern Redemption* (Waco, TX: Baylor University Press, 2019).

R Sender, S Fuchs and R Milo, 'Revised Estimates for the Number of Human and Bacteria Cells in the Body,' *PLOS Biology*, 14(8), 2016, 1-14.

R Sibbes, *The Complete Works of Richard Sibbes* (Vol V) (A B Grosart (ed) London: James Nisbet and Co, 1863).

K Sonderegger, *Systematic Theology Vol 2: The Doctrine of the Holy Trinity—Processions and Persons* (Minneapolis, MN: Fortress Press, 2020).

J A von Werdenhagen, *Psychologia Vera* (Amsterdam: Jansson, 1632).

R Williams, *Being Human: Bodies, Minds, Persons* (London: SPCK, 2018).

R Williams, *Looking East in Winter: Contemporary Thought and the Eastern Christian Tradition* (London: Bloomsbury Publishing, 2021).

Notes

1 Careful attention to detail in the original language is important: God as the creator here is referred to in the personal form (YHWH-God), who alone can make the dust live and breathe. The human (*ha'adam*) is formed from ground/soil (*ha'adamah*). The Spirit (*ruach*) animates the dust (*'aphar*) of the ground (*'aphar min ha'adamah*), but this is not exclusive to humans (Gen 1.20). To be animated by the same spirit is to be animal. Thus, what distinguishes the humans from other animals is neither matter nor life-giving Spirit but being made in the Image of God.

2 A R Johnson, *The Vitality of the Individual in the Thought of Ancient Israel* (Cardiff: University of Wales Press, 1964, second edition) pp 2, 37.

3 W D Davies, *Paul and Rabbinic Judaism: Some Rabbinic Elements in Pauline Theology* (London: SPCK, 1979, third edition) pp 17–21. Paul does use and engage with elements of Greek thinking and culture in some of his letters, but it is a wholly other thing to say that he imbibed and subscribed to their philosophies.

4 P Gooder, *Body: Biblical Spirituality for the Whole Person* (London: SPCK, 2016) p 53.

5 E Radner, *A Profound Ignorance: Modern Pneumatology and its Anti-modern Redemption* (Waco, TX: Baylor University Press, 2019) p 71.

6 *ibid,* p 11.

7 St Augustine (~419), *On the Soul and its Origin* (Book IV) Chapter 19 [XIII].

8 K Sonderegger, *Systematic Theology: Vol 2, The Doctrine of the Holy Trinity—Processions and Persons* (Minneapolis, MN: Fortress Press, 2020) p 538.

9 Tertullian, *De Anima*, chapter 10.

10 D Kelsey, *Eccentric Existence* (Vol I) (Louisville, KY: Westminster John Knox Press, 2009) p 309.

11 John Calvin, *Opera quae supersunt omnia: Epistolicus Calvianus* (Vol IX) (trans G Baum) (Saxony: C A Schwetschke et filium). In Letter 248, John Calvin wrote this in his letter but it was also on his wax seal which he used to close his letters.

12 The image of God must be separate from flesh, otherwise it cannot be immortal and cannot properly reflect the image and likeness of God. J Calvin, *Institutes of the Christian Religion* Vol I (Louisville, KY: Westminster John Knox Press, 1960) p 153.

13 *ibid*, 1.5.5, p 57.

14 M A Lapine, *The Logic of the Body: Retrieving Theological Psychology* (Bellingham, WA: Lexham Press, 2020) p 142.

15 J Calvin, *Institutes of the Christian Religion Vol I* (Louisville, KY: Westminster John Knox Press, 1960) p 54.

16 R Sibbes, *The Redemption of Bodies—The Complete Works of Richard Sibbes* (London: James Nisbet and Co, 1863) p 162.

17 J Calvin, *Institutes of the Christian Religion Vol I* (Louisville, KY: Westminster John Knox Press, 1960) p 192. 'We have already taught that the soul is an incorporeal substance...it dwells there as in a house.'

18 *ibid*, p 155.

19 *ibid*, p 136.

20 The 'magisterial use of reason' happens when we allow reason to stand over and above Scripture as a judge over the word of God. The ministerial use of reason describes the submission of reason as a gift of God to serve (as a minister to) the text of Scripture as the word of God.

21 The fear of ill-fitting speculation was a major motivation for Musculus to reject philosophical methods. Johann Angelius von Werdenhagen is exceptionally harsh in his *Psychologia Vera* (1632). In yet untranslated Latin he writes, 'Oh how foolish mortals we are (to) ask for wisdom from strangers outside Christianity from both pagan and ethnic Greece...(saying) 'Let us create the teachers of God, our own informers: out of the darkness we desire to kindle the light out of the dead' pp 54–55.
22 The Olah offering is always the whole animal (Leviticus 9; Matt 26.6–13).
23 'Be Not Entangled again in a Yoke of Bondage,' *The British Friend, 1*(1), 158 (July 1892).
24 J Behr, 'Nature Makes an Ascent from the Lower to the Higher: Gregory of Nyssa on Human Distinctiveness,' *Zygon*, 58(2), 2023, 550.
25 W J Jennings, *The Christian Imagination: Theology and The Origins of Race* (New Haven, CT: Yale University Press, 2010) pp 1–4.
26 D Bonhoeffer, *Creation and Fall* (Vol 3) (J De Gruchy (ed), (trans) D S Bax) (New York: Fortress Press, 2004) p 77.
27 *ibid*, p 76.
28 *ibid*, p 76.
29 *ibid*, p 77.
30 *ibid*, p 79.
31 K Barth, *Church Dogmatics III/2 (*Edinburgh: T and T Clark, 1960, second edition) pp 344–345.
32 K Barth, *Church Dogmatics III/2 (*Edinburgh: T and T Clark, 1960, second edition) p 360.
33 *ibid*, p 349.
34 *ibid*, p 352.
35 *ibid*, p 393.
36 E Böhl, *Dogmatik* (T Schirrmacher (ed)) (Bonn: Reformatorischer Verlag, 2019) p 193. 'The Bible shows us body and soul as the constitutive moments of the human being.'
37 K Barth, *Church Dogmatics III/2 (*Edinburgh: T and T Clark, second edition, 1960) p 393.
38 *ibid*, p 376.
39 *ibid*, p 339.
40 See also Daniel De Haan, Oxford University and Léon Turner. Look out for the upcoming work of Rebekah Wallace, University of Winchester and Jessica Wyatt at University of Oxford.
41 Sender, Fuchs and Milo, 2016: https://bbc.co.uk/news/health-43674270
42 R Williams, *Being Human: Bodies, Minds, Persons* (London: SPCK, 2018) p 6.
43 *ibid*, pp 57–58.
44 *ibid*, p 62.
45 *ibid*, p 62.
46 *ibid*, p 63.
47 Genesis 18.27: 'Then Abraham spoke up again: 'Now that I have been so bold as to speak to the Lord though I am nothing but dust and ashes.'
48 Before he sees everything clearly through Jesus, observe what the blind man sees in the first stage of healing in Mark 8.22–24.
49 For reflection on these themes specifically as practical metaphors, see also Joy Clarkson's *You Are a Tree* (Bloomington, MN: Bethany House Publishers, 2024).
50 Athenagoras, *De Resurrectione. 15, 6.*
51 P Gooder, *Body, op cit,* p 69.
52 R P Lawson, *Origen: The Song of Songs Commentary and Homilies* (Westminster: Newman Press, 1957) pp 266, 320.